Blackout!

Chicago, Illinois

 Raintree

© 2006 Raintree
Published by Raintree,
A division of Reed Elsevier, Inc.
Chicago, Illinois

Customer Service 888–363–4266

Visit our website at www.raintreelibrary.com

Printed and bound in the United States by Lake Book Manufacturing, Inc

10 09 08 07 06
10 9 8 7 6 5 4 3 2 1

Library of Congress Cataloging-in-Publication Data
Claybourne, Anna.
  Blackout: Sound energy / Anna Claybourne.
    p. cm. -- (Fusion)
  Includes bibliographical references and index.
  ISBN 1-4109-1916-1 (library binding-hardcover) --
ISBN 1-4109-1947-1
(pbk.)
  1. Electric power failures--Juvenile literature. I. Title.
II.
Fusion
(Chicago, Ill.)
  TK1010.C633 2005
  621.319--dc22
                                    2005011082

Acknowledgments
The author and publishers are grateful to the following for permission to reproduce copyright material: Corbis Royalty-free pp. 28 mid, 28 top; Corbis pp. 4–5 (Craig Aurness), 8–9 (Thom Lang); Getty Images p. 14–15; Getty Images/PhotoDisc pp. 16–17, 28 bottom; Harcourt Education Ltd/Tudor Photography p. 12–13; Photonica pp. 26–27 (Michelle Zassenhaus); Rex Features/Sipa Press pp. 20–21; Science Photo Library pp. 6 (Oscar Burriel), 18–19 (Simon Lewis), 22–23 (Cordelia Molloy), 24–25 (Larry Mulvehill).

Cover illustration and interior illustrations by Darren Lingard.

The publishers would like to thank Nancy Harris and Harold Pratt for their assistance in the preparation of this book.

The paper used to print this book comes from sustainable resources.

Contents

Some words are printed in bold, **like this**. You can find out what they mean on page 30. You can also look in the box at the bottom of the page where they first appear.

The Lights Are Out!

It is the worst storm you have ever seen. Thunder rattles the windows. Lightning streaks across the sky. You can hear creaking and crashing noises in the distance. Then, suddenly, the lights go out. The **electricity** has been cut off!

Have you ever wondered what life would be like without electricity? We use it for so many different things. We would feel lost without it.

Electricity is a type of **energy**. We use it to power things such as lights, heaters, TVs, and computers. Some buses and trains work on electricity, too.

Electro Fact!

Energy is the ability to do some kind of work. That could be making things move, heating things up, or making light or sound.

electricity type of energy

It's a Blackout!

When the **electricity** supply is cut off, it is called a power outage or a blackout. The lightbulbs do not work. The TV screen goes blank. Your computer screen is dark, too. Why has everything stopped working?

▲ *The lights have gone out and everything is quiet. All you can hear is the storm.*

Things such as electric lights, TVs, and computers have metal wires inside them. Electricity works by flowing in a **current** along the wires. The electrical **energy** flowing through things makes them work.

Yet what happens if the electricity supply is cut off? Then, electrical energy cannot flow through the wires. Electrical things, such as lights, do not work.

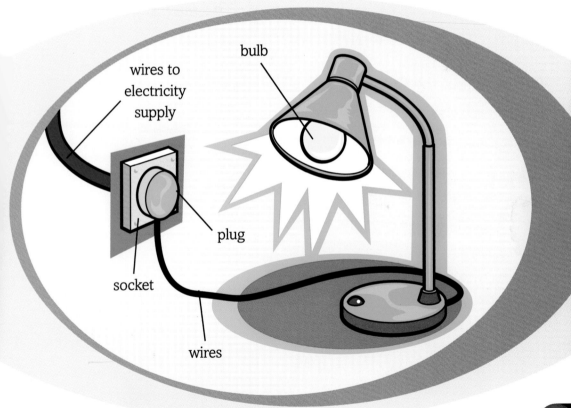

wires to electricity supply

bulb

plug

socket

wires

▲ *A lamp works when electricity flows from the socket along the wires and through the bulb.*

What are you going to do?

current flow of electricity

Get a flashlight!

There are no lights on in your neighborhood. This means that the problem is bigger than the power source in your own house. You have an idea! You can use your flashlight. This is because a flashlight runs on **electricity** that comes from a **battery**.

Electricity will flow from a battery. Yet it can only flow if it has somewhere to go—and then come back again! The path for electricity is called a **circuit**. (The diagram on page 9 shows how an electrical circuit works.)

You dig out the flashlight and press the switch. The bulb flashes on. Now, you can see your way around.

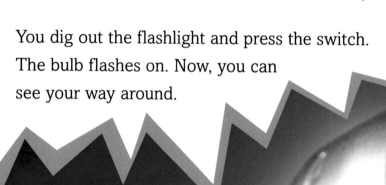

battery small supply of electricity
circuit   loop that electricity can flow around

▼Batteries supply a small amount of electrical **energy**. It is enough to make a flashlight bulb glow. Electricity flows around the flashlight in a loop called a circuit.

1

Electricity flows from the batteries.

2

It flows to the bulb, making it glow.

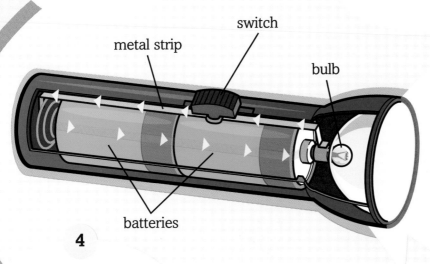

switch

metal strip

bulb

batteries

4

Then, it flows back to the batteries. This completes the circuit.

3

From the bulb, it flows along the metal strip.

Time to find out what is happening . . .

Testing, testing

You decide to check to see if the **electricity** really is off throughout your house. You and your older sister run around. You both flick all the light **switches** on and off. You test all the electrical machines. Nothing comes on. You need to find out why . . .

Switches turn lights, TVs, and other electrical gadgets on and off. When you turn a switch on, it closes up a small gap in the loop of wire called an electrical **circuit.** The electrical **energy** can flow freely around the whole circuit. This makes the gadget work.

When you turn a switch off, the gap opens again. This breaks the circuit. When the circuit is broken, electricity cannot flow. The gadget goes off.

switch   something that is used to open or close an electrical circuit

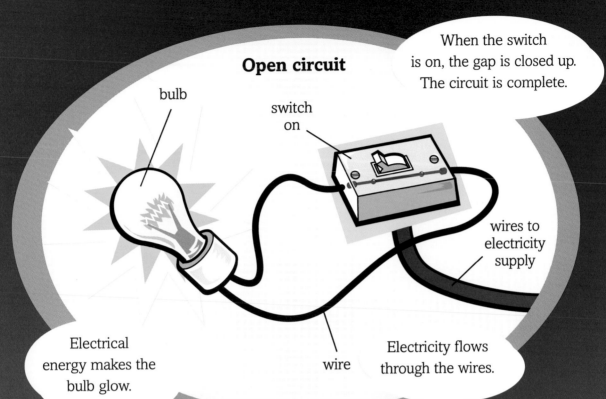

Open circuit

bulb

switch
on

When the switch
is on, the gap is closed up.
The circuit is complete.

wires to
electricity
supply

Electrical
energy makes the
bulb glow.

wire

Electricity flows
through the wires.

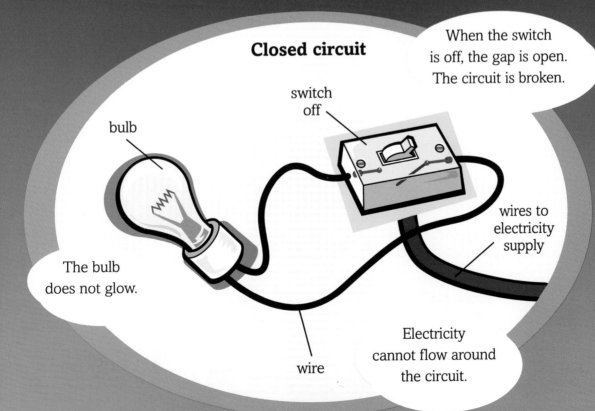

Closed circuit

switch
off

bulb

When the switch
is off, the gap is open.
The circuit is broken.

wires to
electricity
supply

The bulb
does not glow.

11

wire

Electricity
cannot flow around
the circuit.

Battery power

Your sister **switches** on the TV to see if the news is on. She forgot it would not work. You have another idea. You can get the news from your **battery**-operated radio. You find it and switch it on.

Just as the news begins, the sound starts to get quieter. Then, the radio goes silent. What is wrong with it? Oh no! The radio's battery has run out!

"Here is the news . . . "

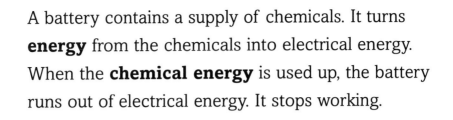

A battery contains a supply of chemicals. It turns **energy** from the chemicals into electrical energy. When the **chemical energy** is used up, the battery runs out of electrical energy. It stops working.

Are you ever going to find out why the lights are off?

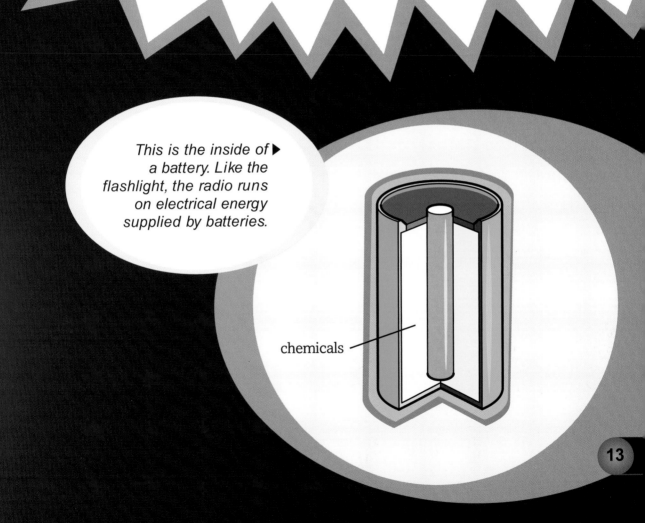

This is the inside of ▶ a battery. Like the flashlight, the radio runs on electrical energy supplied by batteries.

chemicals

13

The Lines Are Down

You take the **battery** out of the flashlight and put it into the radio. Now, at last, you can find out what is going on.

The voice on the radio says that a storm has torn down some power lines. These power lines carry **electricity** to your neighborhood. So, that is what has happened! The electricity is off all over your town. No one knows when it will come back on.

The electricity supply comes from factories called **power stations**. It flows along a huge **circuit** of thick wires, or cables, to homes, offices, and schools. Just as in a smaller circuit, it has to keep flowing to work. If the circuit is broken, the electricity stops.

When a storm tears down ▶ a power line, it puts a gap in the circuit. No electricity can get through to homes or other buildings.

14

power station factory where fuel is turned into electricity

Mom should be home by now. Where is she?

Stuck in a tunnel

There is a good reason why Mom is not home yet. She is stuck underground in a subway train tunnel. Hundreds of other passengers are stuck there with her.

The subway runs on **electricity**. The electrical **energy** flows in a **current** along the metal rails of the train track. It flows to big electric motors under the train. The rails act like the thick cables that carry electricity to your house.

Subway trains ▶ run on electricity. When the electricity stops, the trains stop, too.

Electro Fact!

The world's first electric underground trains ran in London in the year 1890.

How is everyone
going to get out?

Escape!

The passengers are going to have to escape along the tunnel. The driver leads the way with his flashlight. Everyone walks carefully down the side of the tunnel.

They do not touch the electric rails. If the **electricity** came back on, the rails could be dangerous. Metal wires and rails can **conduct**, or carry, electricity.

The human body can conduct electricity, too. You should never touch a wire or rail that has electricity running through it. The electricity can flow through your body. This can give you an electric shock.

In houses, electrical wires are covered with **insulators**. Insulators do not conduct electricity. Rubber and plastic are insulators. They cover electric wires and keep you safe.

A long way home

At last, the train passengers find their way to the subway station. They get out onto the street. But Mom still has a long walk home. It is cold, wet, dark, and stormy, and nothing is working!

Shop lights and cash registers are off. Coffee machines are not working. No one can get a hot drink. The street lights and the traffic lights have all gone out, too. There are traffic jams everywhere.

It is hard for Mom to find her way home. Luckily, she has that key-ring flashlight that you gave her for her birthday. It works with a **battery**. She **switches** the flashlight on. It helps her to find her way.

Electro Fact!

A big blackout hit the northeast of North America in 2003. Thousands of people got stuck far away from their homes.

◄Thousands of people will have to find their way home on foot.

21

What will Mom find when she gets home?

In the Dark

Mom finally opens the front door and comes in. She is freezing cold and soaked through. Her flashlight **battery** is running out.

There is only one thing to do. You all search around for candles. You put the candles in candlesticks and jam jars. This is to make sure that they do not fall over. Then, you light the candles with matches.

Thanks to the blackout, ▶ you have gone back in time 200 years. You are using candles as lights.

You eat your dinner by candlelight. It is a peanut butter sandwich, since the bread and peanut butter do not need to be chilled or cooked. Afterward, you do your homework by candlelight.

It is not easy! You have to sit very near the candles. Even then, it is hard to see. This is what it was like for everyone before **electricity** was invented.

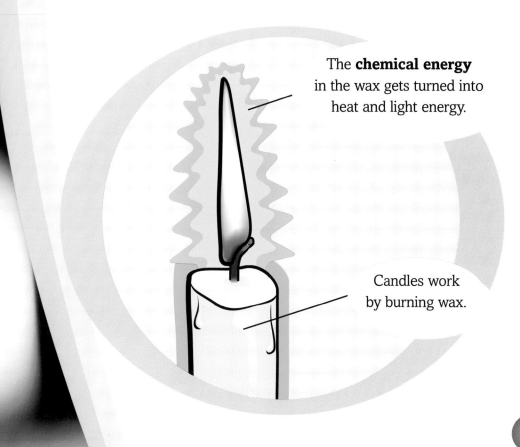

The **chemical energy** in the wax gets turned into heat and light energy.

Candles work by burning wax.

Shutdown!

The blackout goes on all night and into the next day. **Engineers** try to fix the power lines as quickly as possible. It takes a long time.

Meanwhile, you learn to live without lights, the TV, your computer, and all the other electrical gadgets in your house. School is closed. Nothing is working there, either. Shops are shut. Traffic lights do not work. Electric trains are not running.

What about hospitals? They need **electricity** to run their life-saving equipment. Luckily, they have machines called **generators**. Generators make electricity.

> ## Electro Fact!
>
> *A generator is a machine that turns **energy** from fuels, such as gasoline or diesel, into electricity. Heat from burning the fuel powers the generator and produces electricity.*

engineer   someone who designs or understands machines
generator   machine that turns fuel into electricity

▼The hospital is extra busy. Lots of people have had accidents in the dark. It is important for hospitals to have a back-up supply of electricity.

25

Back to Normal

It is getting dark again. It is nearly time for another cold dinner by candlelight. Then, suddenly, there is a flicker. You are blinded by bright yellow electric lights!

◀ At last, everything is working again! There is so much to do. You can watch TV, surf the Web, or even make some hot soup!

You hear your computer starting up in the other room. The refrigerator starts humming again and the TV comes on. You change channels to find the news. The blackout is over! The power lines have been fixed. **Electricity** is flowing again.

This time you were lucky. The electricity was only off for a day or two. What if it was off for days, or even weeks?

Electro Fact!

A lot of electricity is made by burning **fossil fuels**. These are fuels such as natural gas, coal, and oil. But the world's fossil fuels are running out. Scientists are working on new ways to make electricity.

Electrical Inventions Timeline

Most of the electrical gadgets that we have today were only invented in the last 150 years. This timeline shows some of them.

1854 Light bulb

1881 Metal detector

1893 Toaster

1908 Washing machine

1907 Electric vacuum cleaner

1920 Hairdryer

1910 Neon lights

1925 Television

1936 Electric blanket

1928 Electric shaver

1947 Microwave oven

1946 Cell phone

1958 Video game

1956 Video recorder

1964 Computer mouse

1975 Home computer

1978 CD player

1850
1860
1870
1880
1890
1900
1910
1920
1930
1940
1950
1960
1970
1980
1990
2000

Circuit Quiz

Can you name the different parts of this circuit?

Answers

1. Battery   2. Wire   3. Bulb   4. Switch

Glossary

battery small supply of electricity. There might be batteries in your alarm clock or TV remote control.

chemical energy energy stored in chemicals. Fuels such as coal, oil, and candle wax contain chemical energy. So do the chemicals in a battery.

circuit loop that electricity can flow around. All electrical items contain wires arranged in a circuit.

conduct to allow electricity to flow. Metal wires can conduct electricity.

current flow of electricity. If an electric current flows through you, you get an electric shock.

electricity type of energy. Energy from electricity powers all kinds of things, from pocket flashlights to machinery in factories.

energy something we use to do work. Energy comes in many different forms, such as electricity, heat, and light.

engineer someone who designs or understands machines. Engineers use their knowledge of science to make sure machines work.

fossil fuels fuels found in the ground, such as coal, oil, and natural gas. They are slowly running out.

generator machine that turns fuel into electricity. Emergency generators can supply electricity for hospitals during blackouts.

insulator something that cannot conduct electricity very well. We cover electric wires with insulators to make electrical gadgets safer to use.

power station factory where fuel is turned into electricity. Power stations provide electricity for towns and cities.

switch something that is used to open or close an electrical circuit. When a switch is turned on, the circuit is closed. Electricity can flow.

Want to Know More?

Books to read

- Cooper, Christopher. *Electricity: From Amps to Volts*. Chicago: Heinemann Library, 2004.

- Gardner, Robert. *Electricity and Magnetism Science Fair Projects Using Batteries, Balloons, and Other Hair-Raising Stuff*. Berkeley Heights, N.J.: Enslow, 2004.

  An older reader can help you with this book.

- Wyborny, Sheila. *Electricity*. Farmington Hills, Mich.: Gale Group, 2003.

Websites

- http://www.energyquest.ca.gov/
  Learn more about how energy lights our homes, powers our trains, and keeps our radios and televisions turned on. Check out this cool site from the California Energy Commission.

- http://www.smud.org/safety/world/
  Find out more about where electricity comes from and how it travels. You'll also find games and quizzes related to electrical safety.

Energy comes in lots of different forms and can be used to do all sorts of things. To see some of them, check out *Wackiest Machines Ever*.

What will happen in the future if we run out of fuel and cannot make enough electricity? Find out in *The Future – Bleak or Bright?*

Index